KEITH TYSON
NATURE
PAINTINGS

TULLIE HOUSE
MUSEUM AND
ARTS SERVICES
CARLISLE

Keith Tyson
Nature Paintings

Published to coincide with an exhibition at
Tullie House Museum & Art Gallery
20 September – 30 November 2008

Exhibition and publication curated and organised
by Fiona Venables, Tullie House Museum &
Art Gallery, Carlisle, UK

Published in 2008 by
Tullie House Museum & Art Gallery
Castle Street, Carlisle, CA3 8TP
T: 01228 618718
www.tulliehouse.uk

ISBN: 978-0-907852-18-6

Designed by AW @ www.axisgraphicdesign.co.uk

Set in Monotype Bell and John Baskerville Sans
Printed by Gutenberg Press, Malta

Photography of works by Prudence Cuming Associates Ltd
and Dawkins Colour
Endpapers: Scafell Pike from Upper Eskdale
Photograph by Stephen Hewitt

Distributed by Art Data @ www.artdata.co.uk

Tullie House Museum & Art Gallery is owned and managed
by Carlisle City Council.

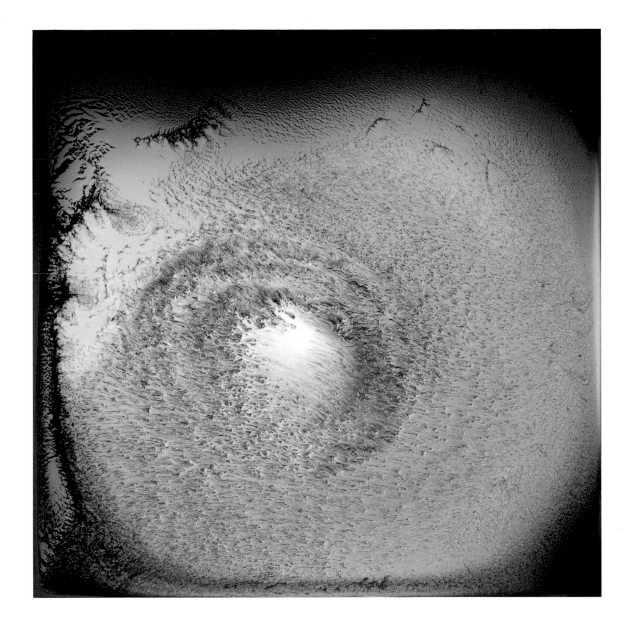

Nature Painting, 2008

Mixed media on aluminium
610 x 610 mm
'To Think Yes' collection, London

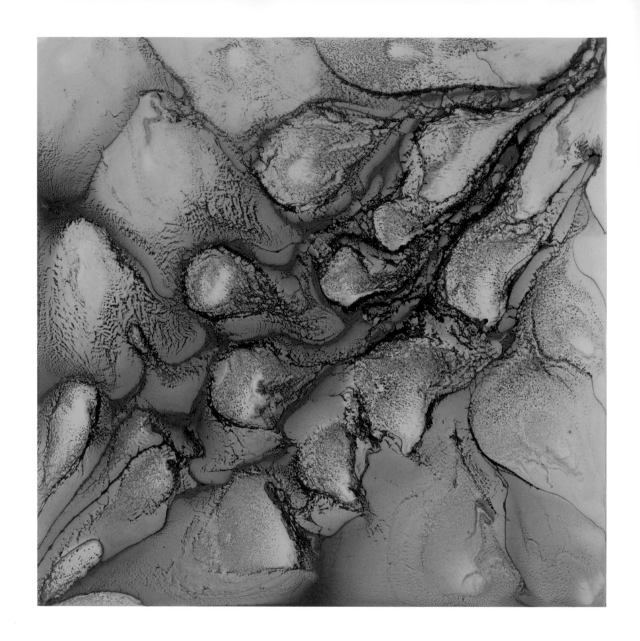

Nature Painting, 2008

Mixed media on aluminium
610 x 610 mm
'To Think Yes' collection, London

Nature Paintings

Cumbria is a county that remains closely associated with the rise of Romanticism in the late 18th century and with the poets and artists who lived in or visited the Lake District over two hundred years ago. These artists took inspiration from the drama of the region's 'beauty, horror and immensity' (Dr. John Brown speaking of the Keswick area in around 1753[1]) and sought to convey, through words and imagery, the power of Nature over man as embodied in the county's mountainous land masses.

Keith Tyson was born in Ulverston in 1969, on the edge of the Lake District National Park. He studied engineering in Barrow-in-Furness and began his art training at Carlisle College of Art (now the University of Cumbria). The artist attributes his love of the natural world to his Cumbrian upbringing and claims that many of his happiest childhood memories are of walking near his grandfather's hill farm between Ulverston and Windermere. So it is Tyson has chosen Cumbria as the backdrop to this, the first exhibition of Nature Paintings in the UK.

Standing in front of these works, one cannot help but be struck by their beauty. Conceptual art is rarely spoken of in such terms; one of its principal tenets has been to denounce the preoccupation with the visual, to emancipate the idea from the object. Yet Tyson does not see a contradiction between the two things. In an interview with the artist Dave Beech in 1998, he said:

> I think I suffer to a certain extent from that phenomenon whereby if it doesn't look like conceptualism or it doesn't have the hallmarks of it, then it is not considered as such ... Mine tend to be manifestations as opposed to representations. It is about what brought them into being. It's usually

1   From a letter to Lord Lyttelton.

about all the complex things that occur before the work exists. I've got nothing against the visual. I don't believe the art exists outside the object. The work's final manifestation is this object, which is readable.[2]

The difficulty in reconciling the beauty of Nature Paintings with their conceptual basis is compounded by a tension between the automatic visual allusions the paintings make to the natural world – including cell structures, geological strata, topography, the cosmos – and the method of their making. We are conditioned to value skill – including that of the painter in mastering his medium to represent the physical world. Yet skill has been subjugated to chance in the rendering of Nature Paintings. Their forms and colours are determined, not by the artist's governing hand, but by the reactions between paints and chemicals when combined and poured at different angles and temperatures onto aluminium plates.

Unlike his 18th and 19th century forebears, Tyson is not interested in capturing the power of Nature through any form of mimicry. As Gabriel Ramin Schor points out[3], these works are neither real, nor imaginary, nor fantastic portrayals of Nature. The paintings are innocent of any meaning or value we may bestow upon them. They are images without model. They are manifestations of Nature being allowed to return to itself.

So, is common ground to be found between the conceptual 21st century artist and the Romantic painters of the past? Gabriel Ramin Schor has described Tyson as a 'Neo-Romantic wanderer between the planes of reality, possibility and probability.' The sense of discovery artists must have felt on first encountering the Cumbrian mountains two hundred years ago has been lost in part through the popularisation of the region as a tourist destination and the familiarisation of its vistas through endless reproduction. Ruskin lived long enough to witness and bemoan his beloved Lake

2 See *Another Tyson Ear Bending: Dave Beech talks to Keith Tyson*, Everything Magazine, 1998.
3 See *Keith Tyson: Nature Paintings*, Haunch of Venison, 2007.

District become tamed by the tides of tourists for which he was, in part, responsible. Much is made of Tyson's interest in science and its formal systems of classification, but it can be argued that the artist uses scientific language primarily to reclaim this impulse for discovery. Science offers a fertile ground for him to explore the potentiality of the unknown. When I asked the artist how he responded to the label of 'Romantic', he replied:

> 'Romantic' is an interesting term, because it originally comes from an anti-enlightenment movement. The Romantics advocated the emotional and irrational, whereas I don't think that there's a contradiction between the rational and the emotional. I feel that I'm trying to create a synthesis between the two; I'm not really into binary opposites.
>
> I like the idea of being interested in science, nature and process, and also being interested in the emotional and romantic significance of those things – what are the emotional effects of relativity? That is the kind of ground I want to explore, the outer and inner world. I see it very much like Taoism or Buddhism, an exploration of external and internal phenomena to find out what is left behind after you've looked at all the possibilities.

The philosopher AC Grayling argues that, for most of history, humans have believed that the possession of language and reason set them apart from the rest of Nature. Although the ancient Greeks, including Aristotle, argued against this philosophy it was not until Renaissance times when the idea that man was an integral part of Nature really came into its own. 'Today's science', Grayling says, 'has confirmed this Renaissance intuition. We know from biology and genetics how much we are part of Nature, and how much all the things that were once thought to distinguish humankind from other animals are in fact widely shared by them'.[4]

Whereas, 200 years ago, the Cumbrian mountains must have

---

4 See *Pursue Pleasure: It's the natural way to do good in the world*, The Times, March 18, 2007.

seemed indomitable to the artists who visited, today our recognition
of Nature's power is equalled, if not surpassed, by that of its
vulnerability. The term 'ecology', meaning the relations of organisms
to their environment - including other organisms - did not in fact
enter the English language until 1873. Advances in imaging
technology used in scientific study - from films of microscopic
organisms to satellite pictures from space – and their wide
dissemination via television have had a particularly powerful bearing
on this rising ecological awareness. They also affect how we read
Nature Paintings. When I asked Keith Tyson about exhibiting this
series of work within the context of Tullie House, a museum housing
collections of both Art and Natural History, he said:

> A lot of the work is reminiscent of certain structures, such as cell
> formations, mountains and trees, and so on and so forth, and the same
> forces of Nature that created those forms are sort of replicated in these
> paintings. It wasn't intentional, but I think there's a very interesting
> connection there. And the idea of looking around the natural history part
> of the museum, and then seeing these paintings, where you can identify
> various similarities or could even see them as **species** of paintings, makes
> this a very nice context to show them.

Certainly, surrounded by Nature Paintings I am reminded of one
of those films in which all natural life appears to be encompassed,
in which the camera pans rapidly outwards from a single cell, to
microscopic life forms, to humans, to continents, until you are
looking down on Earth from space. Likewise, the art critic Michael
Archer has compared Tyson's work to the doodles a child makes
on the inside cover of his science folder when bored in class, or his
penchant for extending an address from street name and city, to
country, world, and ultimately the entire cosmos[5].

5 From a review of the exhibition 'Supercollider' at South London Gallery, Art Forum, March 2002.

I'm interested, Tyson says, in exploring the origin of things, the origins of me, of you, of the art that I make. Why does something come into being? It is a question I've asked over and over again. It comes from my own psychological dynamic of when I was a child, thinking 'why am I here?' In that sense, I'm a very traditional artist, I think. I have produced work that currently isn't seen as traditional but I think actually is. Its aim is to explore what we are.

Keith Tyson has been producing Nature Paintings since 2006. Asked whether an end to the series is in sight, the artist is ambivalent. Of course, authorship can never entirely be eradicated from these paintings' making. Editorial decisions are inevitably made in terms of the position the artist assumes in pouring chemicals, or in the selection of paint. He is adamant however that the most successful works are the ones where he has been at his most detached, where he has trusted in Nature. And, as long as Nature continues to create works of seemingly infinite variety, who is he to curtail it? I will give the final word to the artist:

I think the reason people find [Nature Paintings] beautiful is because they're reminiscent of what we are – the deepest dynamic, just maths and energy and thermal dynamics. When you look at the Earth from above, you're struck by how incredibly detailed it is and how effortlessly Nature reveals these things to us. I just want to do the same in my paintings I suppose.

Fiona Venables
Tullie House Museum & Art Gallery

Unless otherwise credited, all quotes by Keith Tyson are taken from an interview with Fiona Venables for Select in Furness Magazine, Issue 3, September 2008.

Nature Painting, 2008

Mixed media on aluminium
610 x 610 mm

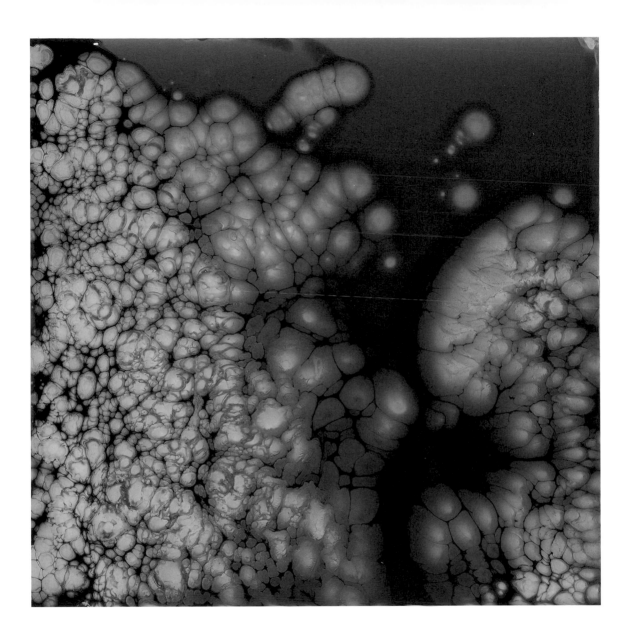

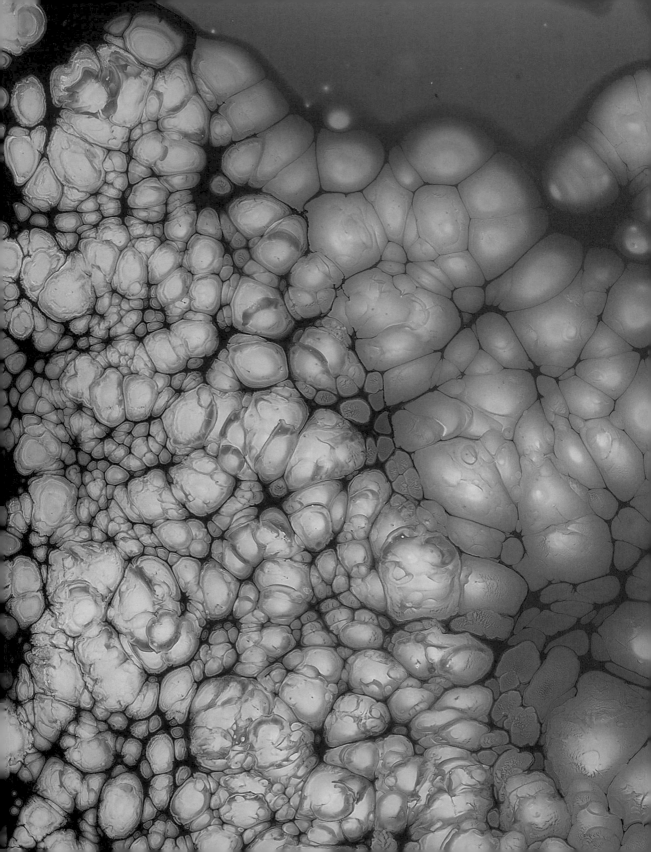

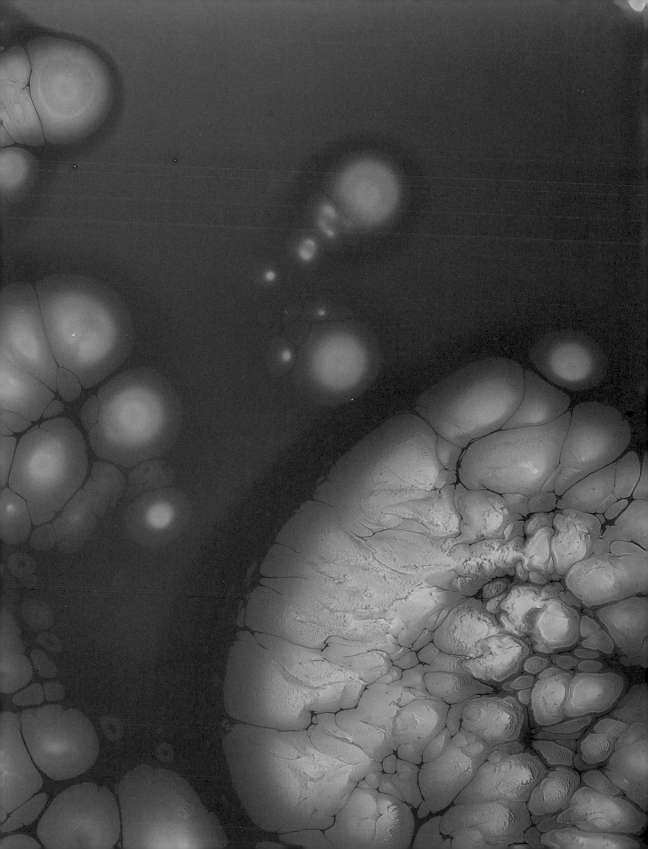

Nature Painting, 2008

Mixed media on aluminium
1490 x 1490 mm

Nature Painting, 2008

Mixed media on aluminium
1220 x 1220 mm
'To Think Yes' collection, London

Nature Painting, 2008

Mixed media on aluminium
610 x 610 mm

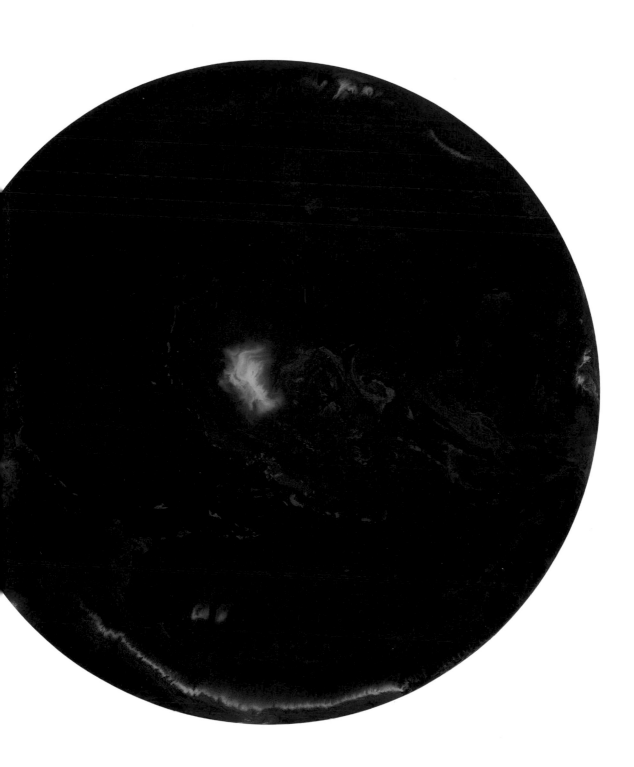

PREVIOUS SPREAD

Interacting Galaxies
(Nature Painting), 2008

Mixed media on aluminium
1990 x 3695 mm
Courtesy of ProjectB Contemporary Art, Milan

Nature Painting, 2005

Mixed media on aluminium
610 x 610 mm
'To Think Yes' collection, London

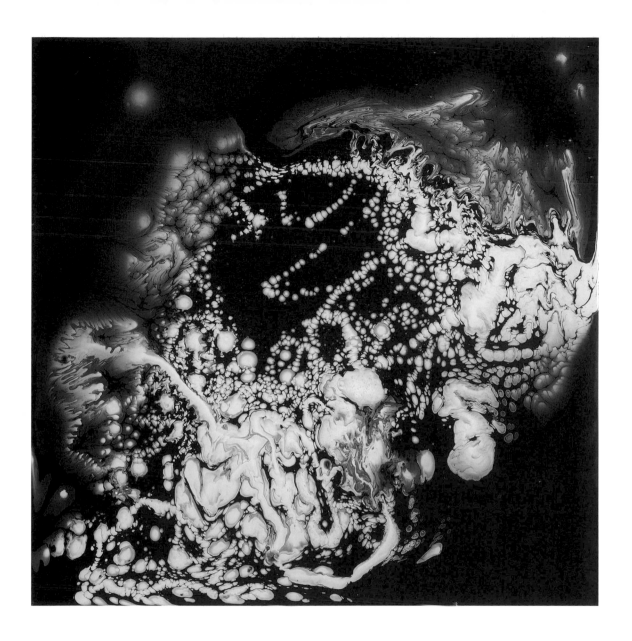

Nature Painting, 2008

Mixed media on aluminium
1220 x 1220 mm

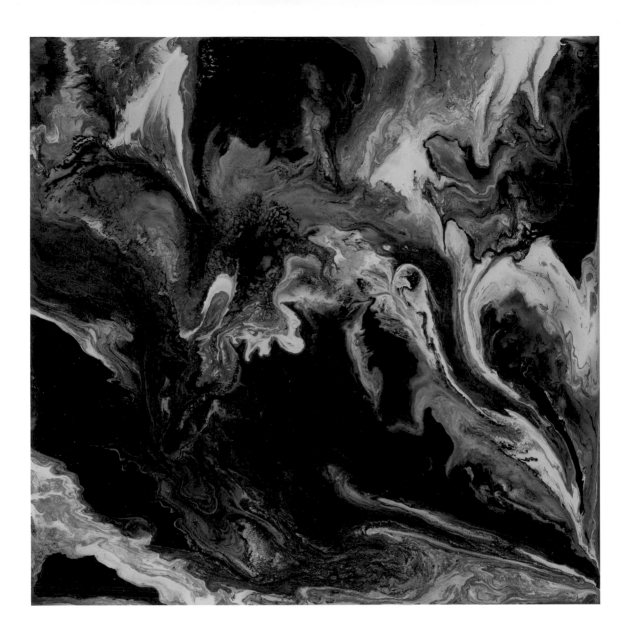

Nature Painting, 2008

Mixed media on aluminium
610 x 610 mm
'To Think Yes' collection, London

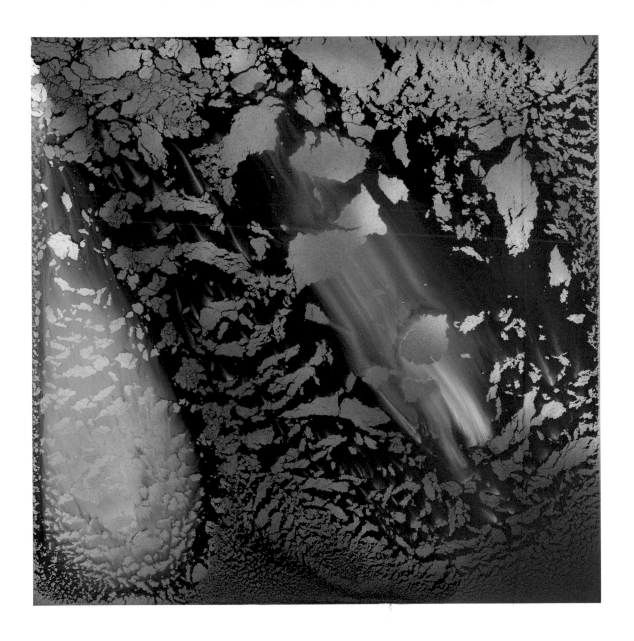

Positive Streamer (Nature Painting), 2008

Mixed media on aluminium
920 x 5490 mm (triptych of three equal parts)

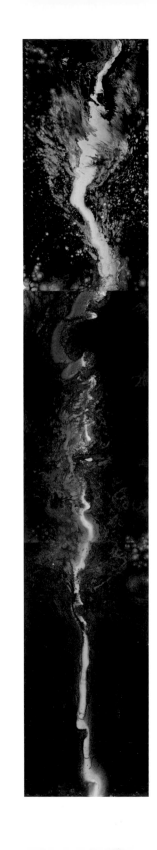

Nature Painting, 2008

Mixed media on aluminium
610 x 610 mm

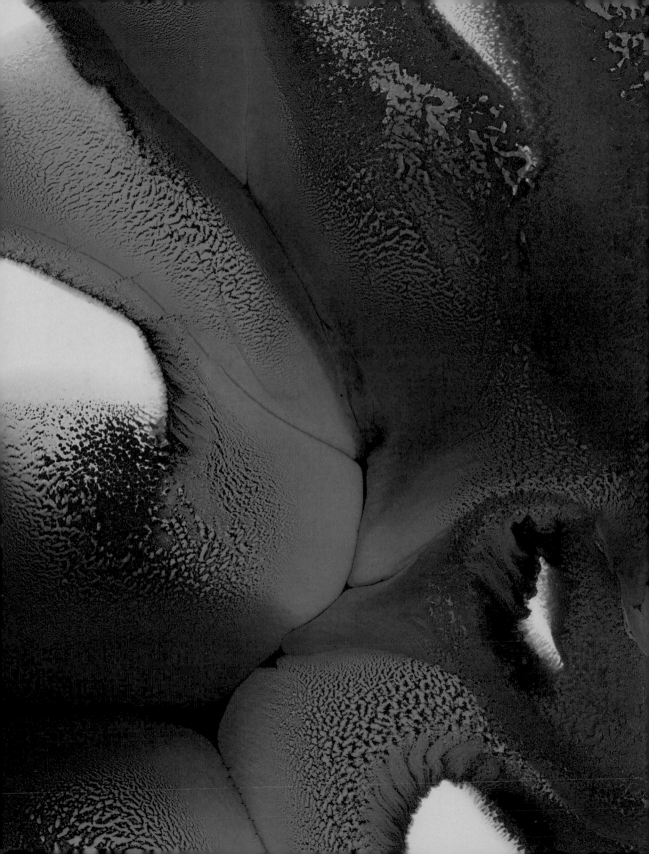

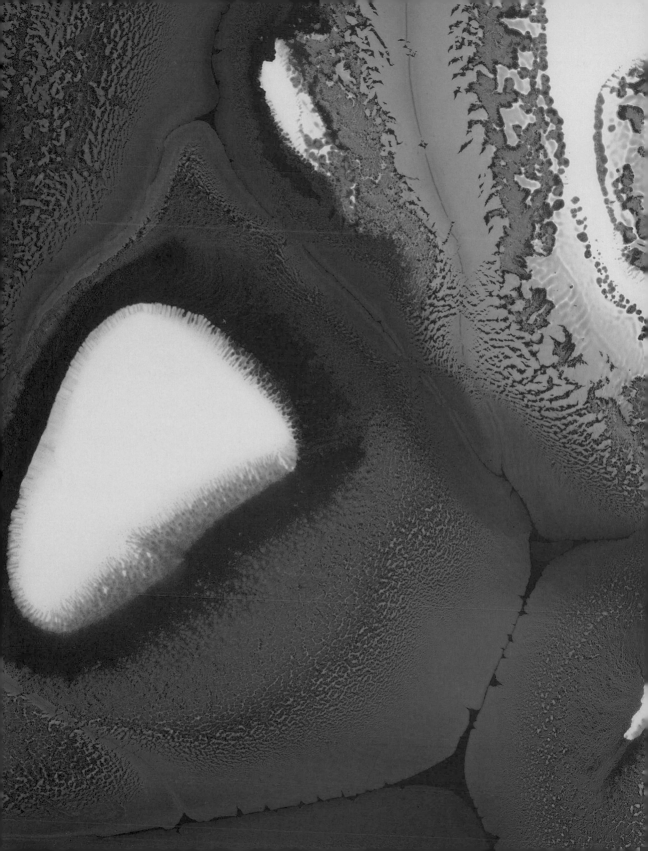

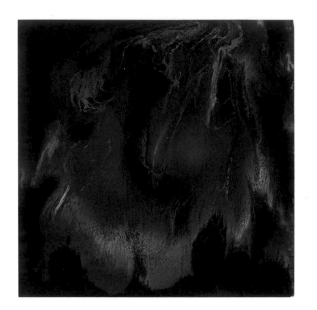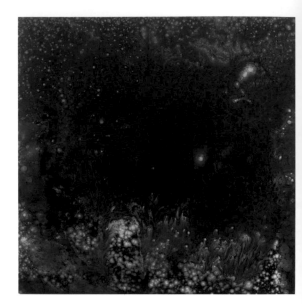

Four Elements (Fire) (Water) (Earth) (Air)
(Nature Painting), 2008

Mixed media on aluminium
1980 x 7920 mm (comprised of four equally sized panels)

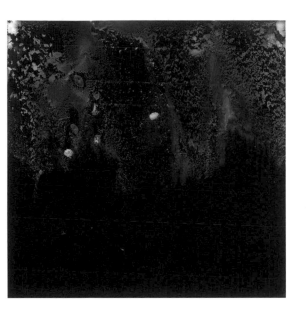 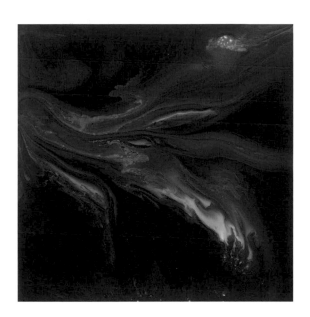

Nature Painting Planet, 2008

Mixed media on aluminium
1220 mm diameter
'To Think Yes' collection, London

Nature Painting, 2008

Mixed media on aluminium
610 x 610 mm

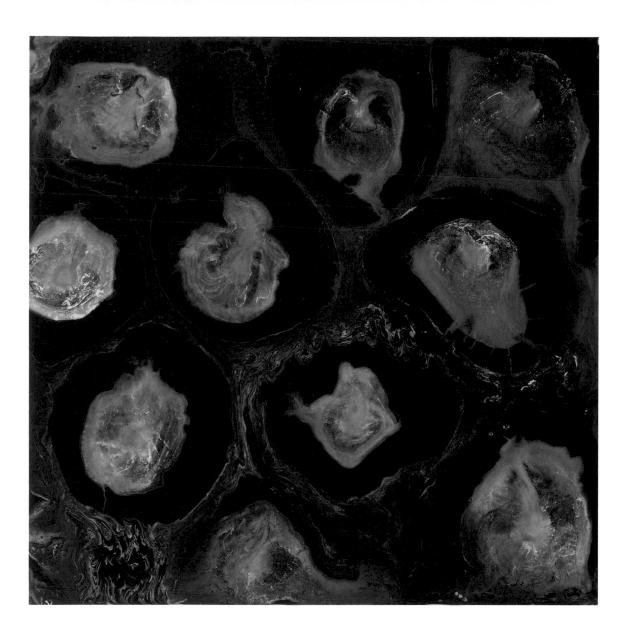

Nature Painting, 2008

Mixed media on aluminium
1490 x 1490 mm

Nature Painting, 2008

Mixed media on aluminium
610 x 610 mm
'To Think Yes' collection, London

Nature Painting Mirror, 2008

Mixed media on aluminium
1220 x 1220 mm
'To Think Yes' collection, London

Nature Painting, 2008

Mixed media on aluminium
610 x 610 mm
'To Think Yes' collection, London

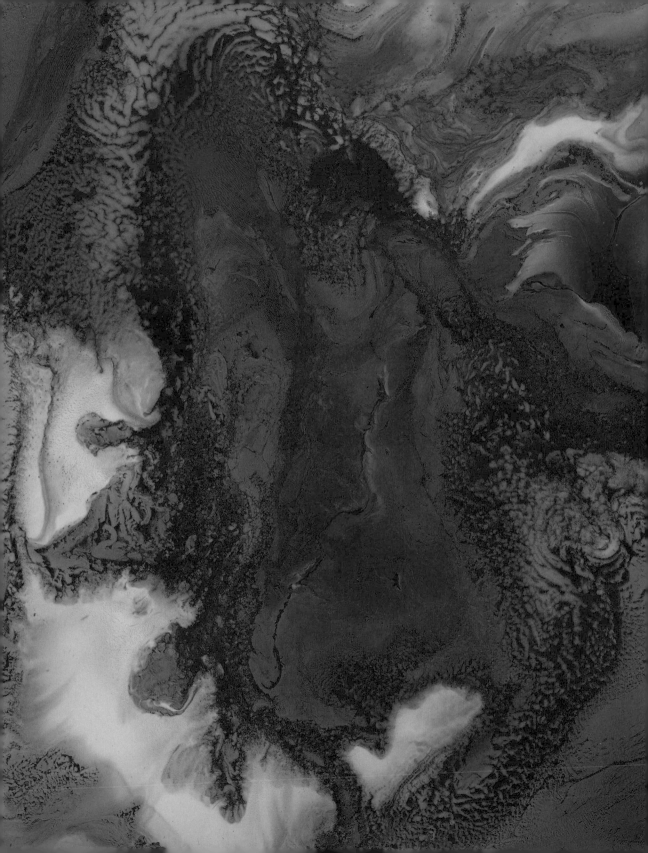

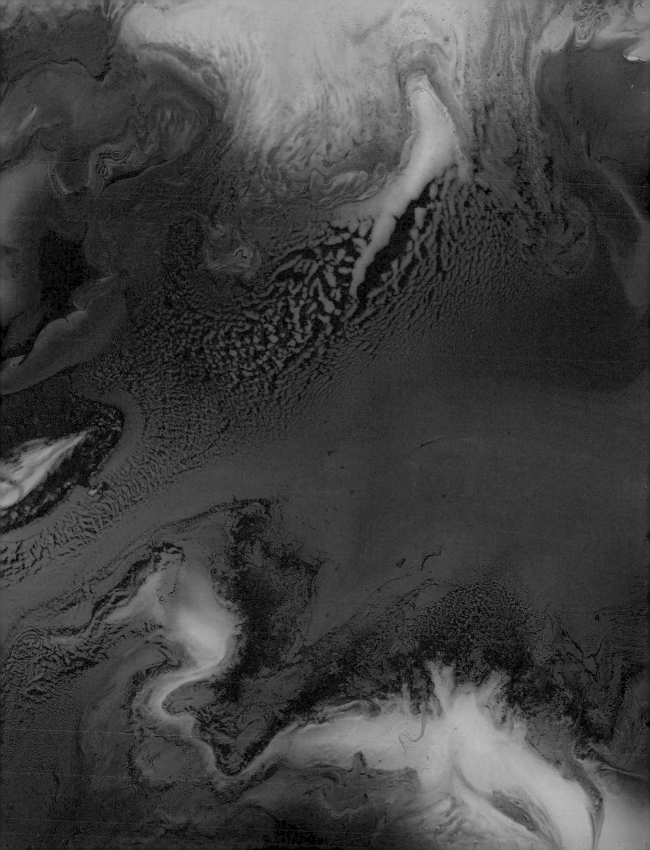

Keith Tyson

1969   Born in Ulverston, UK

Education
1990 – 93 University of Brighton: Alternative Practice BA
1989 – 90 Carlisle College of Art
1984 – 89 Barrow-in-Furness College of Engineering: M.E.C.S (Mechanical Engineering Craft Studies)

Awards
2007   Professorship, University of Brighton, UK
2005   Honorary Degree of Doctors of Letters, University of Brighton, UK
2002   Turner Prize, London, UK
1996   ICA Arts and Innovation Award, London, UK

Selected Recent Solo Exhibitions
2008   *Random Nature*, Project B, Milan, Italy (catalogue)

2007   *Studio Wall Drawings 1997 – 2007*, Haunch of Venison, London, UK (catalogue)
Keith Tyson, Large Field Array, PaceWildenstein, New York, USA (catalogue)
Keith Tyson, Large Field Array, De Pont Museum, The Netherlands (catalogue)

2006   *Keith Tyson, Large Field Array*, Louisiana Museum, Denmark (catalogue)
Keith Tyson, Nature Paintings, Haunch of Venison, Zurich, Switzerland (catalogue)
Keith Tyson, The Sum of All Possible Paths, Galerie Vallois, Paris, France

2005   *Keith Tyson*, The Bates College Museum of Art, Maine, USA
Geno Pheno II, PaceWildenstein, New York, USA (catalogue)

2004   *Geno Pheno I*, Haunch of Venison, London (catalogue)
The Terrible Weight of History, Galerie Judin, Zurich, Switzerland (catalogue)

2003   *Collected Short Stories*, Galerie Vallois, Paris, France
Works for a Teleological Accelerator, Arndt and Partner, Berlin, Germany

2002 *Keith Tyson*, Kunsthalle Zurich, Switzerland (catalogue)
Supercollider, South London Gallery, London, UK (catalogue)

2000 *Studio Wall Drawings*, Anthony Reynolds Gallery, London, UK
One of Each, Galerie Ursula Krinzinger, Vienna, Austria (catalogue)

Selected Recent Group Exhibitions

2008 *History in the Making: A Retrospective of The Turner Prize*, Mori Art Museum, Tokyo, Japan
Beyond Measure: Conversations Across Art & Science, Kettle's Yard, Cambridge, UK (catalogue)
Estratos, Murcia, Spain (catalogue)
Martian Museum of Terrestrial Art, Barbican, London, UK (catalogue)

2007 *Oeuvres Encombrantes*, Gallerie Vallois, Paris, France (catalogue)
Turner Prize Retrospective, Tate Britain, London, UK
Reconstruction II, Sudeley Castle, Gloucestershire, UK (catalogue)
Aggression of Beauty, Arndt and Partner, Berlin, Germany

2006 *You'll Never Know: Drawing and Random Interference*, Hayward Gallery Touring Show, London, UK (catalogue)
How to Improve the World: 60 Years of British Art, Hayward Gallery, London, UK (catalogue)

2005 *Logical Conclusions: 40 Years of Rule Based Art*, PaceWildenstein, New York, USA (catalogue)
Dionysiac, Centre Pompidou, Paris, France (catalogue)

2004 *'Is there a Curator to Save the Show?'*, Galerie Vallois, Paris, France
Another Zero, Galleria d'Arte Moderna e Contemporanea, Bergamo, Italy (catalogue)

2003 *Outlook*, Athens, Greece (catalogue)
Independence, South London Gallery, London, UK
Home, Galerie Vallois, Paris, France
Thatcher, Blue Gallery, London, UK
Micro/Macro: British Art 1996 – 2002, Mucsarnok Kunsthalle, Budapest, Hungary (catalogue)

Talking Pieces, Museum Morsbroich, Leverkusen, Germany (catalogue)
The Lost Collection of an Invisible Man, Laing Art Gallery, Newcastle upon Tyne, UK

2002   *Turner Prize Exhibition*, Tate Britain, London, UK (catalogue)
Comer o No Comer, Centro de Arte de Salamanca, Salamanca, Spain (catalogue)
Strike, Wolverhampton Art Gallery, Wolverhampton, UK
Public Affairs, Kunsthaus Zurich, Switzerland (catalogue)
Reality Check, Wharf Road, London, UK; House of Artists, Zagreb, Croatia;
Gallery Rudolfinum, Prague, Czech Republic; Bunkier Gallery, Krakow, Poland;
Mucsarnok Kunsthalle, Budapest, Hungary (catalogue)
Con Art, Site Gallery, Sheffield, UK (catalogue)
25 Sao Paulo Biennial, Sao Paulo, Brazil (catalogue)
Flights of Reality, Kettle's Yard, Cambridge; Turnpike Gallery, Leigh, UK (catalogue)

2001   *Brave New World*, Galeria OMR, Mexico City, Mexico (catalogue)
L'effet Larsen – associative networks, O.K Centrum fur Gagenwartskunst, Linz,
Austria; Casino-Forum d'Art Contemporain, Luxembourg (catalogue)
Open Plan P3, The Marathon, Alphadelta Gallery – Artio Gallery, Athens, Greece
(catalogue)
Nothing, Northern Gallery for Contemporary Art, Sunderland, UK; Contemporary
Art Centre, Vilnius, Lithuania; Rooseum Malmo, Malmo, Sweden; Mead Gallery,
Warwick, UK (catalogue)
The Fantastic Recurrence of Certain Situations: Recent British Art and Photography,
Sala de exposiciones del Canal de Isabel II, Madrid, Spain (catalogue)
Berlin Biennale, Berlin, Germany (catalogue)
49 Biennale de Venezia, Venice, Italy (catalogue)
makeshift, University of Brighton Gallery, Brighton, UK (catalogue)
Century City: Art and Culture in Modern Metropolis, Tate Modern, London, UK
(catalogue)
2000   *The British Art Show 5*: Edinburgh; Southampton; Birmingham; Cardiff, UK
(catalogue)
Domestic Pairs Projects, Kunsthaus, Glarus, Switzerland
Over the Edges, SMAK- Stedelijk Museum voor Actuele Kunst, Gent, Belgium
(catalogue)
Dream Machine, Hayward Gallery, London, UK (catalogue)

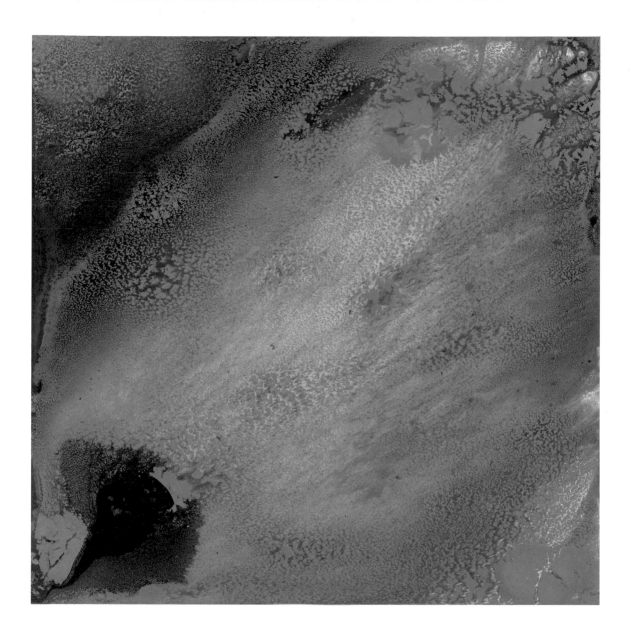

Nature Painting, 2005

Mixed media on aluminium
610 x 610 mm

Nature Painting, 2008

Mixed media on aluminium
1490 x 1490 mm
'To Think Yes' collection, London

Acknowledgements

Tullie House Museum & Art Gallery wishes to thank Keith Tyson for presenting Nature Paintings in Carlisle and for being so generous with his time in all aspects of the exhibition's organisation. We thank Arts Council England North West, Northern Rock Foundation, Friends of Tullie House, Cumbria County Council and Renaissance North West for their financial support of both exhibition and publication. We thank everybody at Tullie House who has been involved with the exhibition's organisation with particular mention to be made of Amy Walker, David Clarke, Mick North, Melanie Gardner, Hazel Fenton and Catherine Rogers. We also extend a sincere thank you to the following organisations and individuals for their involvement with the exhibition:

Arndt and Partner, Berlin
Artists First Management
Galerie Vallois, Paris
Haunch of Venison, London
Pace Wildenstein, New York
ProjectB Contemporary Art, Milan
Keith Tyson Projects

Jade Awdry, Emanuele Bonomi
Anika Carpenter, Nick Dowdeswell
Jo Hardacre, Gill Hedley
Calum Sutton, Alan Sykes
Richard Wadhams, Alan Ward

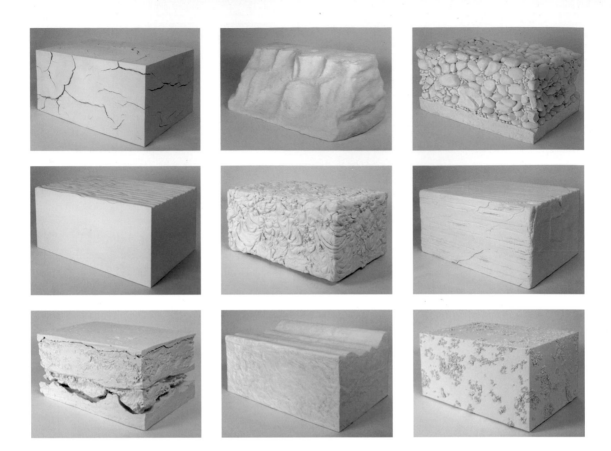

Nature Sculptures, 2008

Polyester resin
9 parts, each approx. 915 x 600 x 450 mm